ISBN: 1497422000
ISBN-13: 978-1497422001

DEDICATION:

This book is dedicated to all those who had to suffer under centralized state-run Semashko health systems and aims to liberate people's health in those places where Semashko is still in place.

Foreword: The Georgian Model: Market-Based Healthcare as a Game-Changer in Developing Economies
by Frederik Cyrus Roeder

Healthcare expenditures are rising globally, and policy makers are looking for a cure. In most cases, either more centralization or rationing have been prescribed to tackle this problem.

Nations with more planned economies are especially struggling to adjust their domestic health systems to market realities. Most post-communist countries still lag behind the industrialized world in health outcomes and also experience a high degree of corruption and informal payments.

Over the course of the past eight years, the Republic of Georgia's health system developed a unique approach towards health reform and has experienced great success so far. Formerly one of the most dysfunctional and corrupt countries to receive care in Europe, Georgia has emerged as the leading health system in the sphere of post-Soviet powers.

Georgia broke the old reform paradigm of gradual change and instead introduced bold, market-based reforms in a short time period that the country's healthcare system largely hadn't seen before.

Post-communist countries provide a good case study on how a big government stake in healthcare affects the availability and affordability of services. Centralized and so-called "free" health systems tend to have global budgets for services. Such ex-ante allocation of funds causes a misallocation of resources and thus shortages in many areas of care. This results in the long queues that can be seen not only in many Eastern European health systems but also in the single-payer systems of the United Kingdom and Canada. The absence of private property and lack of incentives gives rise to highly disengaged medical and nursing personnel.

These conditions often leave patients in a situation where they don't receive the "free" care they need. As a result, patients are motived to look for ways to incentivize doctors and other providers to treat them. Such incentives usually have a monetary character and are either called "informal payments" or "bribes."

A very illustrative example of how expensive "free" healthcare can become is the Romanian health system. The World Bank estimates that Romanians spend 75% of their entire family's monthly income for informal payments during a hospital stay. One IMAS market research survey showed that 85% of Romanians believe they won't receive standard care if they don't bribe the medical staff. Private healthcare providers with modern wards and superior care often charge patients less than corrupt doctors in "free" hospitals do. As a result, a parallel private hospital system emerged that offers patients much better care for the same amount of money or less.

Eastern European policy makers — most prominently in Poland, Slovakia, and the Czech Republic — have come to understand the deficiencies of government-run healthcare and appreciate the growing importance of private healthcare provision and funding.

The Republic of Georgia recently underwent one of the world's most radical health reforms, all within just a couple of years. The World Health Organization once ranked the Georgian health system among the worst in the world. The provision of "free" healthcare was shaped by ubiquitous corruption. Reformers led by then Minister of Economics, Kakha Bendukidze, decided to abolish the dysfunctional Soviet-style single-payer system.

Insurance vouchers for the poor and elderly replaced government health insurance. These vouchers cover the purchase price of a basic benefit package from a private health insurance company. Private health insurance companies compete for these patients and the remaining population who can either purchase insurance or can remain uninsured. There is no individual mandate. As a result of these market reforms, private insurance companies and hospital chains have built more than 100 modern inpatients facilities within the last three years.

Within half a decade, Georgia's total restart of its healthcare system created positive results for patients. Health indicators such as infant mortality and life expectancy rose dramatically. Informal payments went down from 40% of the country's health expenditures to below 5%. Georgian hospital experts estimate that prices went down by 40% due to the reforms. Competition and private enterprise created a diverse landscape of hospitals, health maintenance organizations, insurance plans, and freedom of choice. This pluralistic competitive system allows ongoing innovation driven by patients' needs. The liberalization of the Georgian health system attracted foreign investors that didn't solely inject capital into the system but also brought know-how from abroad.

It's not just transitioning economies that are moving towards more private healthcare. Sweden and Germany, often seen as democratic socialist role models, have facilitated a huge surge of private healthcare in the last few years. After two decades of privatization, for-profit companies own almost 40% of German hospitals. By contrast, the American Hospital Association estimates that merely 20% of hospitals in the US are for-profit. Privatization of hospitals allowed significant improvements in quality of care. Efficiency gains reduced treatment costs, providing better care at a lower cost.

The sad truth is countries that experiment with socialized medicine often experience catastrophic levels of care, high levels of corruption, and a misallocation of scarce resources. Time and again, patients will try to opt-out of those systems or pay for parallel private services. In response, many countries have started implementing policies to strengthen the private sector, introduce more freedom of choice, and allow competition. The results have been a vast improvement in the availability and quality of healthcare for citizens.

This book showcases the experiences of two leading healthcare reformers from Georgia, former Minister of Economics Kakha Bendukidze and former Minister of Health Andria Urushadze. Michael D. Tanner from the Cato Institute in Washington, D.C. also contributes his external view on the Georgian reforms. These experts' experiences written down in this publication shall serve as a roadmap for policymakers to enact successful healthcare reform in Eastern Europe and beyond.

Chapter 1: Initial Situation of the Georgian Health System

by Andrew Urushadze

The Way Out from Soviet Healthcare

Over the last few decades, the Georgian health system has experienced several different stages of transformation. Georgia became an independent nation with the dissolution of the Soviet Union in 1991, but unfortunately still has the roots of many problems of the past.

Before 1991, Georgia's health system operated on a Soviet model, where care was supposedly free and universal. Unfortunately, many Georgians today foster false nostalgia for the supposedly sweet Soviet times, believing that healthcare system was well-funded at no charge to patients, provided equal opportunity for treatment, and maintained high moral standards.

For many years, Soviet propaganda trumpeted the supposed superiority of socialized medicine and the inevitability of its triumph over the capitalist order. Today, a more accurate analysis of health data illustrates that the stagnation of Georgia's economy and problems with its health sector had started long before its independence in 1991.

Soviet sympathizers will claim that healthcare was among main policy priorities of the Union of Soviet Socialist Republics (USSR), but the reality is that the health system was deteriorating and increasingly suffered from lack of funds before 1991. For many years, the USSR was the only industrialized country where the percentage of gross domestic product (GDP) being spent on the health of its people decreased.

During the period of stagnation under General Secretary Leonid Brezhnev's regime, the health system was plagued by a series of increasingly serious problems that especially came to attention during the perestroika restructuring period of the late 1980s. In the final years of the USSR, national healthcare expenditures were merely 3% to 4% of GDP. This was only half the average of countries in the Organisation for Economic Co-operation and Development (OECD) at the time. Health expenditures as a share of the national budget fell from 9.8% in 1955 to

10

6.6% in 1965, then from 5.2% in 1978 to 4.3% in 1986.[1] After the USSR's disbandment, the newly independent satellite states inherited medical care systems that were in a chronic state of disarray.

Because of continual underfunding, Georgia's healthcare system slipped into critical condition and continued to deteriorate. Despite the fact that over half of the health facilities had been built before 1940, the government allocated funds towards the construction of new facilities instead of upgrading or even maintaining existing ones. In 1988, 115 facilities were under construction, most of which remain unfinished today.

The lack of necessary medical equipment and misuse of human resources also became an acute problem in the years before reform. Georgia had over 120,000 persons employed in the health sector. The density of doctors was one of the highest in the world at 1 physician per 197 inhabitants. Undertrained, under-utilized, and inadequately managed healthcare professionals greatly inhibited the efficiency and effectiveness of Georgia's healthcare services.[2]

The notion of equity in health is closely linked with the idea of social justice grounded in redistributionist principles.[3] According to Soviet legislation, every citizen had equal access to treatment. In actuality, as much as half of central health budget of the USSR was allocated to finance a so-called "fourth department" of the Health Ministry that provided care exclusively to political elites who accounted for less than 1% of the population. The remaining 99% had to survive in a health system that merely spent 1.5% to 2% of GDP — a fraction of the total 3 of 5% of GDP in total health spending over the last years of socialist medicine.

Even in 2001, funding allocations for the health facilities of Georgian Ministry of Internal Affairs was almost three times more than for general public clinics. The bureau received funds in a bloated, budget-item basis, just like they did in the USSR. According to the applicable rules and regulations, these funds could be utilized for the needs of ministry personnel and, in some cases, their family members as well[4].

According to the economist Yuri Maltsev, government bureaucrats and Communist Party officials realized that the USSR's supposedly egalitarian health system was not efficient at providing care to the masses as early as 1921, only three years after Lenin's nationalization of medical care. So, as in all countries with socialized medicine, a two-tier system was created — one for the masses and the other for the bureaucrats and their intellectual servants with much better service. In the USSR, it was often the case that while workers and peasants would die in state hospitals, the medicine and equipment that could save their lives was sitting unused in facilities reserved for the government elite.[5]

The sad truth is that under the supposedly egalitarian Soviet system, some patients were more equal than others.

Corruption

The USSR's inefficient bureaucracy and permanent fiscal deficit were fruitful ground for corruption and created a shadow economy, particularly in the healthcare system.

Medical services were officially free of charge, but were nonetheless accompanied by a well-developed system of informal payments to ensure proper care. Such tipping was not perceived as corruption, as it was accepted by both patients and doctors. For ideological reasons, the salaries of medical professionals were lower than other specialists, so informal payments had to compensate the difference. In some cases, reimbursements to hospital staff were made by patients returning favors through various kinds of gifts. By pulling medical resources out of circulation, the shadow economy worked precisely against the very people who need help most — the poor.

This informal economy of healthcare was unfortunately the norm in most Soviet republics. Most physicians in Soviet Estonia also received extra payments from their patients in the form of gifts or cash tips on a fairly regular basis[6]. In Russia, these types of supplemental payments to physicians were called "thank you money." In Asian republics, corruption in health facilities was accepted as a way of life.

From a Western perspective, such payments to physicians are easily seen as bribes to obtain preferential access to care. In reality, these informal payments were essentially an unofficial fee-for-service mechanism that developed under the former Soviet system.[7]

However, illegal payments were not the only form of corruption. Budget funds to provide healthcare, purchase new equipment, hire new personnel, and maintain a sufficient supply of medicine were driven by bribes and gifts.

Even in post-soviet Georgia, these practices were largely extended and partly get legitimization.

Quality of Care

As if the bureaucratic troubles with the Soviet healthcare system weren't bad enough, the USSR's approach to medicine was very different than Western, evidence-based medicine. Diagnostic criteria were often different, and many drug treatments and physical therapies were unheard of in the West.

Generally, treatment methods from Soviet times often involved obsolete drugs, long treatments, lots of injections, and low thresholds for hospital admission and surgery. Such a culture of over-diagnosis put patients' health at risk, strengthened drug resistance, made healthcare less affordable, and contributed to the medical poverty trap.

Beginning with the suspension of the Hippocratic Oath at the beginning of the Russian revolution in 1917, the Soviet state "de-professionalized" medicine, emphasizing the doctor's duty to defend the interest of the state rather than of the individual. When the Soviet empire collapsed, some doctors welcomed the opportunity for change. Unfortunately, many others — especially those with sanitary epidemiological training (the Soviet equivalent to public health) — have remained nostalgic about the old methods that assured efficient disease control at the expense of human rights.[8]

Health Outcomes

Low investment, poor morale, and ineffective efforts to improve the health sector's performance
resulted in great stagnation and deterioration of health outcomes during the last decades of the USSR.

Health conditions in the USSR worsened steadily since the mid-1960s. According to 1990 data, the health status of the population in Georgia was relatively poor compared to the rest of Europe. Life expectancy was 68.1 years for men and 75.7 for women, compared to 71 years for men and 78 for women in Western Europe.

The infant mortality rate (IMR) declined by 50% over the previous 30 years, yet remained twice as high as in Western European countries. Poor

prenatal and neonatal care resulted in one-third of all infant deaths occurring in the first three days of life. The maternal mortality rate (MMR) was estimated to be more than four times that in Western Europe[9]
.

In April 1991, Georgia officially declared its independence from the USSR. The country inherited a healthcare system that faced a prolonged professional and financial crisis. The economic troubles directly following the USSR's collapse only worsened the existing problems in the health sector.

During the first years of its independence, Georgia formally retained the principle of "free" access to healthcare inherited from Soviet period. Of course, such free health was only illusion after the collapse of planned economy. This led to a rapid decline in public spending and limited allocation of resources to the health sector. By the end of 1993, economic output fell by up to 78%, as the economic crisis resulted in the collapse of government revenues that also affected resources for the health sector that fell to USD 0.8 per/capita per annum.[10] Government revenues were no longer able to sustain highly inefficient, state-run socialized medicine.

During the first years of independence, health services were formally funded by general revenues. Unfortunately, the economy was in a condition of total collapse, resulting in chronic underfunding of the health system. As the result of shortages in the electricity supply, medical facilities experienced long periods without power, heating, and water. The public salaries paid to medical personnel were largely symbolic, as their annual income was less than the estimate monthly cost living minimum in the country. Private spending became the major source of health sector financing. Patients were obliged to pay the full costs for many services. According to several reports, the population in Georgia paid between 66-87% of the national health bill. Preventive services also broke down, including the virtual collapse in the national immunization program in the early 1990s.[11]

After 1991, the health status of the country continued to deteriorate. The IMR rate had risen by 13%, reaching an estimated 21.4 deaths per 1,000 births in 1993. The MMR likewise increased due to an increasing number of home deliveries. Deaths caused by cardiovascular diseases increased by 35%, and the overall age adjusted mortality rate rose by 18%[12].

First Wave of Health Reforms, 1995-2000

After years of hostilities and social unrest, the parliamentary elections in 1994 and adoption of a new constitution created political and economic stability. In response to the harsh financial crisis, in 1995 government introduced new health reforms, including social insurance, user fees, and new provider payments. The reforms largely concentrated on generating revenue to the desperately underfunded system.

Major reforms included a move to more pluralistic systems of both funding and delivery. Primary health care was strengthened, privatized, and hospitals were streamlined, introducing new arrangements on purchasing and reimbursement of health services. Social services and healthcare were brought closer together through the merger of the Ministries of Health and Social Welfare in 1999.

Economic Context

From 1993 to 1994, Georgia started to experience some economic recovery like most former Soviet powers. Unfortunately, the country quickly found itself trapped in another period of economic turbulence from 1997 to 1998. Russia's continuing civil strife and economic crisis threw Georgia back into economic stagnation and social unrest that did not end until 2001. Consequently, the economic recession in Georgia was deeper and longer than other transitioning economies.

A number of factors contributed to the starkly differing economic evolution between former Soviet satellites and other Eastern European countries during the transition years — namely, corruption, mismanaged privatization, a lackluster rule of law, and geographical distance from the European Union. Working together, these factors led to economic breakdown and rendered the health reforms of the 1990s a complete failure.

Reform Context

Fee-for-service reforms were soon endorsed in the hope that informal payments would decrease. Payments for services not in the Basic Benefit Package (BBP) were legalized and co-payments for some BBP services formalized. Initially, the BBP consisted of nine federal and five compulsory municipal health programs. Since then, this package has gradually expanded to 28 federal and 8 municipal programs. However, the expansion was not accompanied by a corresponding increase in funding. As such, all the state health programs were severely underfunded once again.

In order to respond to the general budget shortfalls and inject additional resources in the health system, the Georgian government instituted a Health-Program framed health system, co-funded by a social insurance model. The burden of the tax was to be shared by employers and employees (3% +1%). Social insurance deficits were supposed to be covered by transfers from general government revenues. Municipal health funds received additional revenues from city budgets. Contributions to the municipal health funds were calculated based on a flat rate per person, depending on the number of people living in the city, but they had to be at least 2.5 Gel.[13] Unfortunately, when the majority of the population is unemployed or self-employed and the revenue administration is corrupt, tax collection is nearly impossible.

Public health expenditures as a percentage of GDP dropped substantially from just over 4% in 1991 to 0.70% in 1998, and further down to 0.59% in 1999. There were similarly low real allocations to the health budget from 1995 to 1998. Only 55% of the health sector budget was executed in 1997.[14] In 2000, approximately $11 per person was budgeted for annual state spending on health, although much less was received than pledged. The funds allocated to oncological services in 1999 covered only about 700 patients, when around 2100 patients were expected to require such services.[15]

Low official reimbursement rates and unawareness of official hospital costs created an environment conductive to shifting the major part of the real hospital costs onto patients, resulting in a high level of informal payments yet again.

According to the World Bank, only about 22% of all healthcare expenditures in 1999 came from government budgets or insurance funds. The health sector remained dependent on private spending paid by patients at the time of service. With an estimated 87% of all health spending coming out of pocket, Georgia had the highest rate of private spending in the region. These high prices caused many families to slip into poverty.

Public vs. Private Health Expenditures in the CIS-7 in 1998:

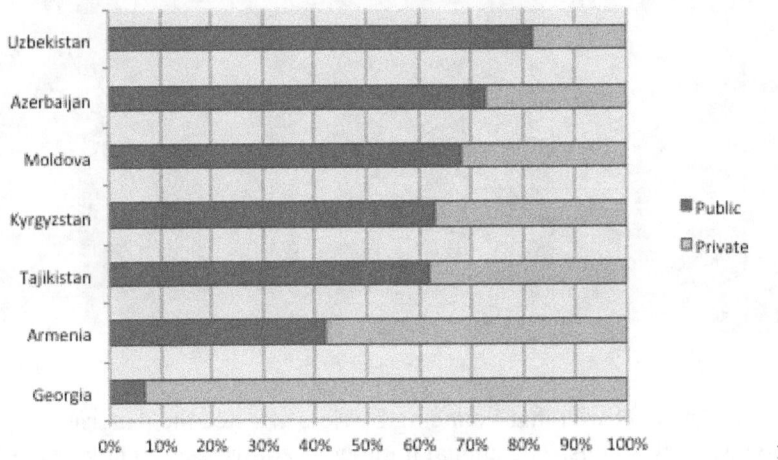

16

Shifting the major financial burden of health expenditure towards private households caused a significant fall in affordability and utilization of health services. Only 46% of those who were sick sought professional treatment, and 20% of those that self-treated themselves did so because they could not afford professional treatment.[17]

In the autumn of 2001, quantitative cross-sectional surveys were conducted in eight former USSR satellites to assess the probability of attending a health professional the previous year. Georgia had the poorest access to healthcare in a comparative assessment of eight former Soviet republics.[18] In Georgia, almost 77.5% of individuals reported were unable to afford or attend a skilled health worker and paid the highest percentage of informal payments during consultations.

In fact, informal payments to doctors and nurses were ingrained in the medical tradition of former USSR countries, dating back to communist times. It is not until the last decade that this practice has largely ended. But they do not seem to have been a matter a concern until the last decade. The highest probability of making an out-of-pocket payment or a gift was in Georgia at 65%.

Percentage of Patients Paying Informally or Making Gift during Most Recent Consultation 2001:

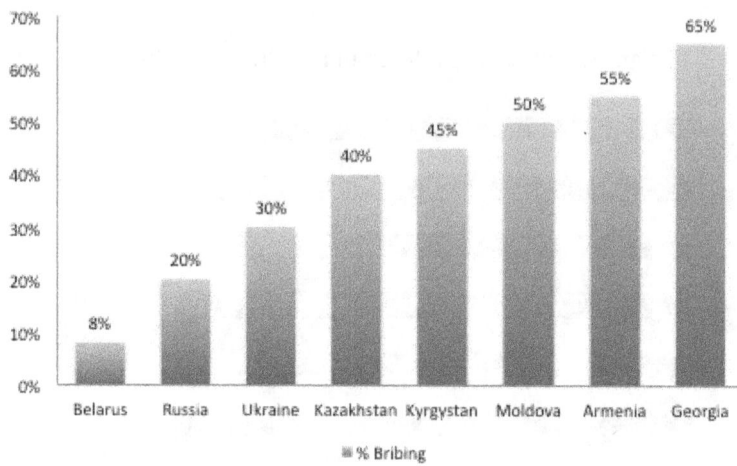

19

The same study showed that financing barriers affected the patterns of admissions to hospitals. The annual number of admissions and average length of stay decreased dramatically over a short period of time, from 15.3 in 1991 to 9.8 for acute care beds in 1997. Consequently, the capacity of the hospital network created in the country during the Soviet times became highly excessive. Occupancy rates became alarmingly low at 27.6%.

A study amongst 41 hospitals in 1999 revealed that most patients were aware of the official service rates in hospitals because the main part of payments was informal at about 60%. In fact, only 20% of Georgians knew that state fund partially paid for their healthcare.[20]

State of Hospitals

Georgia inherited a bulky and obsolete health infrastructure after the collapse of the Soviet Union. The need for streamlining hospitals in Georgia was obvious. The highly inefficient, resource-intensive model forged by Soviet bureaucrats like Nikolai Semashko was too rigid to sustain in a market-based economy.

Communist leaders measured medical achievements by the number of beds and personnel. As a result, an excessive number of beds and medical staff were commonplace. Provider payments were also based on inputs rather than health status or outcomes.

The system was skewed towards secondary care, with a dominant role for hospitals and a proliferation of outpatient specialists working alongside poorly trained generalists in the primary care setting. Medical facilities were all publicly owned. There were no incentives for efficiency, quality of care, or responsiveness to patients. In a highly centralized system, managerial autonomy and management skills were limited and health personnel were narrowly trained.

The number of hospital beds and staff deemed necessary for a local population was relatively high compared to Western Europe. To a large extent, this phenomenon reflected the fact that labor was cheap and easily available, but mostly, because of the nature of the system.

The transitioning years have showed once again that the health sector is an integral part of the socio-economic structure and that it is illusionary to believe that it can remain untouched during persistent economic recession and social degradation.

The former Soviet powers' economic crisis led to substantial cuts in the provider network. The total number of hospitals declined greatly from 402 in 1988 to 272 in 1998 as a result of chronic underfunding. From 1998-99 alone, the actual number of doctors dropped by more than 20% and the number of nurses by 50%. Nevertheless, Georgia had more doctors per capita in 1998 at 3.86 per 1,000 than other Central European and newly independent countries (2.49 and 3.72 respectively).

Although the number of hospitals was cut by some 40% after the first 10 years of independence, the number of hospitals per 100,000 inhabitants was still about twice that of the European Union.

In Tbilisi, there were almost 11,000 beds in 51 hospitals serving a population of 1.28 million. A similarly sized population covered by an American healthcare plan would require only 3,000 beds. Despite the surplus of beds, the majority of Georgian medical facilities were unable to provide good quality of care. The buildings and structures were mostly depreciated and badly suited for medical purposes.

Even as late as 2007, Georgia had one of the lowest acute care hospital admission rates in the World Health Organization's (WHO) European Region at just 6.3 per 100 people. Meanwhile, the average for the EU was 17 per 100 and 20.7 per 100 among countries in the Commonwealth of Independent States (CIS).[21] The average length of stay in acute care hospitals in Georgia was 5.7 days in 2007, which is below the 2006 EU average of 6.5 days and considerably lower than the 2007 CIS average of 11 days.[22]

Low utilization rates, significant excess of medical personnel, and scarcity of financial resources to support the inflated infrastructure called for immediate and radical actions for restructuring of the medical system.

According to the TI Georgia report on Georgian Hospital Sector (2012) the most frequently mentioned problems prior to privatization were:

- Outdated infrastructure.

- A non-competitive environment.

- Inadequacy and low quality of services.

- Weak regulation and enforcement.

- High level of out-of-pocket payments and corruption.

- Unequal distribution of healthcare services throughout the country.

In order to optimize the hospital sector nationwide and achieve the acceptable occupancy rates of 75-80%, the only plausible strategy was liquidating excess beds by 45-50% and optimizing the number and location of medical facilities.

From 1998 to 2000, several efforts were to streamline the number of clinics. However, it was naïve to think that such reforms would be immediately effective considering corruption was deeply rooted in the system and the main stakeholders were uninterested in changing the situation.

Need for Reforms

The need for reforms in the early 2000s was obvious. The health status of the population during the 10 years of independence had severely worsened. Georgia was one of the few countries in the CIS where the important Millennium Development Goals of reducing early childhood mortality and maternal mortality did not exhibit a positive trend.

The WHO estimated[23] that a person born in Georgia in 2003 can expect

to live 71 years on average — 75 years if female and 67 years if male.
The official national figure for the population average is 76.1 years of
life expectancy as of 2001 — 78.7 years if female and 73.5 years if male.
The difference between WHO estimates and national figures is due
mostly to under-registration of child mortality.

Data showed that regularly reported rate of five mortalities per 1,000 live
births in Georgia was about half of the estimated actual rate. Sadly, this
was similar to the underreporting levels in the other countries of the
south Caucasus. As under-registration of child deaths occurs mostly
before the age of one, this discrepancy indicated that infant mortality and
neonatal mortality must be underestimated as well.

Based on nationally reported deaths and births in 2001, there is a
probability that of every 1,000 live births in Georgia, about 27.6 children
would die before age five. Adjusting for the known biases in national
data such as underreporting of vital statistics, the WHO estimated
Georgia's latest probability to be 45 deaths of children under five per
1,000 live births.

In addition, WHO estimated that the mortality rate of children under five
did not changed from 2000 to 2003. The respective rate for the European
Region as a whole decreased at an average annual rate of about 3.5%.[24]

Between 1990 and 2002, Georgia's MMR increased by almost 80%,
peaking in 1997. After that year, the rate fell by 22% until 2002. To
achieve its Millennium Development Goal (MDG) in 2015, Georgia's
MMR would have to fall another 86% according to the WHO.

MORBIDITY AND MORTALITY RATES IN DIFFERENT INCOMES GROUPS (1997)		
AVERAGE MONTHLY INCOME	MORBIDITY LEVEL/1000	MORTALITY LEVEL/1000
< 30 GEL	82	36
30-50 GEL	27	27
50 > GEL	8	2

Annual household surveys in Georgia from 1996 to 2001discovered that
poverty was on the rise and health expenses was one of the main causes.

Many surveys in Georgia have shown that patients need hospital services but often delay treatment because they cannot afford to pay.
In 1998, a National Health Expenditures Matrix was developed for Georgia by consultants from the United States' Actuarial Research Corporation, using 1997 as the base year with projections for the year 2000.

The preliminary matrices showed national spending of 312 million GEL in 1997, 87% of which consisted of out-of-pocket spending. Out-of-pocket spending included cost-sharing for government programs, direct payments for services not covered by the government's programs, and informal payments demanded by providers for services covered by government programs.

The results of a 2000 survey by the State Department for Statistics has shown around 65% of medical care in Georgia is either self-treatment or provided free-of-charge from relatives or neighborhood doctors. 3% is emergency outpatient care, 14.9% is regular outpatient care, and 5.7% is inpatient care. The private sector accounts for 10.4%. The volume of services provided by the state is rather limited, equating to 24.6%.

In Georgia of those who were hospitalized, the poor paid 70% of their monthly household expenditure on the treatment episode and the non-poor paid 60%. 40% of the households in the poorest quintile have reported having to borrow funds or sell their property to finance health expenditures.

In short, a great inequality of health incomes arose in the 1990s. Low-income individuals were exposed to unreasonable levels of morbidity and mortality, as seen in the table below.

Georgia had the lowest level of health service utilization in the Europe and Central Asia Region with less than two outpatient visits per capita and five inpatient visits per 100 people. Being ill increased the probability of becoming poor, as 10% more individuals fell below the poverty line after incurring hospitalization expenditure.

After the failure of the first wave of health reforms, Georgia's poorly managed health system was in a condition of severe collapse. Public enthusiasm for change in the health system was replaced by disillusionment.

Georgian Health Profile 2002

• **Maternal mortality rates increased by approximately 45% between 1990 and 1997**
• **Deaths caused by cardiovascular disease increased by 35%**
• **The overall age-adjusted mortality rate increased by 18%**
• **Declining life expectancy**
• **Increased infant mortality from 7.6 in 1980 to 20.1 in 2002**
• **Increased maternal mortality from 36.0 up to 46.6 in 2002**
• **80-85% out-of-pocket payments**
• **Excessive and obsolete health infrastructure, with 951 outpatient facilities, 114 outpatient hospital departments, and 512 midwife posts in 1998 — of which 5% of ambulatories had basic equipment**
• **2,2491 hospital beds (488,5 beds per 100 000 people, 740 beds per 100,000 people in Tbilisi) in 1999, with 28% occupancy rates in hospitals in 1996-97**
• **1.2 patients a day per physician**
• **Unequal accessibility to health services in rural and urban areas for the different social groups**
• **Dissatisfied and disqualified medical personnel, receiving wages of up to 20 GEL/month in 2003 ($10) and large dependence on informal payments**

Chapter 2: Chronicle of the Georgian Healthcare Reforms

by Andrew Urushadze

To paraphrase Graff Tolstoy, every health system is unhealthy in its own way. Even when different health systems share the same problems (e.g. equity, efficiency, quality, safety, effectiveness of care), each country has its own solution based on unique social, economic, political, and cultural backgrounds.

Before 2003, Georgia's health system went through a number of well-intentioned but poorly implemented reforms. They seemed fine in theory, but not so much in practice. The sad reality is that the early years of Georgia's independence from the USSR in the 1990s failed to improve the poor health outcomes of the Soviet era.

Despite the plethora of evidence demonstrating socialized medicine's ills, opponents of reform stubbornly continued to make anti-market arguments. "Privatization of healthcare is not just wrong," they would say, "it's inhumane and immoral. People's health should not be subject to the profit motive." Fortunately, policy makers saw through the weakness of this argument.

Within a very short period of time, the old Soviet system that so severely damaged the country's health had been replaced with newly constructed, well-equipped modern clinics. A private health insurance system quickly emerged half of Georgians receive state funded health insurance.

Government has radically transformed the health system, moving rapidly from budget-funded direct provision of medical care in public facilities to voucher-based direct customer financing in mostly private facilities. The health sector has since evolved based on competition among private-sector health insurers and providers seeking to maximize their profits by providing quality care.

By minimizing the government's role in the daily administration of health service providers, the Ministry of Health has drastically decreased the cost of the health system's bureaucracy and marginalized corruption in the health sector. A stable regulatory environment has replaced obsolete licensing rules.

Soon, the government began tightening its belt, decreasing administrative costs sharply. Most state agencies were merged or liquidated, decreasing ministerial staff by 60% to minimize bureaucracy. All health agencies moved into one building, freeing up thousands of quadratic meters of state-owned offices in the capital, Tbilisi, for commercial use.

The new healthcare system reflects the numerous remarkable economic and political changes arising out of the Rose Revolution. The health sector's progress was part of the country's bold liberal reforms that freed it from government monopoly and allowed it to benefit from public–private partnerships. Indeed, the health sector's successful transformation was just one of several successful reforms the Georgian government implemented to create a new social-economic order of prosperous market competition.

Privatization of Public Hospitals

The Georgian government's "100 New Hospitals" plan of January 2007 had the effect of a bomb explosion in changing the health landscape. The proposed solution of completely privatizing the hospital sector was truly shock therapy for the country's nearly collapsed hospital infrastructure. After years of indecisiveness, the government informed stakeholders that it was committed to creating better hospital services.

The Hospital Reform Plan, prepared by State Minister of Reforms Coordination Kakha Bendukidze's office was short and clear:

> *We have an excessive and obsolete medical infrastructure, an inefficient financing model, and an inadequate regulatory system. Doctor – Patient - Society - all are dissatisfied with the existing situation. There is public consensus on necessity of radical change. 100 new hospitals countrywide, improved access to high quality health services, improved health of the population that we are expecting after the 3 years of implementation.*[25]

> *Mr. Bendukidze proposed a plan to fundamentally reshape healthcare services throughout the country. Handing the healthcare industry over to the private sector, he argued, would lead to increased competition, increased patient choice, and —*

correspondingly— the provision of higher quality healthcare services.[26]

Hospital Planning

In January 2007, the Georgian government approved the Hospital Development Master Plan. The plan called for the complete replacement of the existing hospital infrastructure within a three-year period from 2007 to 2009 by transferring full ownership rights from the state to the private sector. According to the terms of the current plan, private investors were to supply Georgia 100 new hospitals and 7,800 new beds (4,185 in Tbilisi and 3,615 in the regions).

This plan marked the first time the government not just announced the beginning of the reforms but also presented financial and technical details of its implementation. An estimated 200 million USD were expected to be invested in hospital real estate during first two years and up to 700 million USD in the following five. The total estimated investment needed for a full refurbishment of the hospital sector was 1 billion USD, which amounted to almost 10% of Georgia's GDP in 2007.

The master plan determined Georgia's total hospital capacity and the optimal location for inpatient facilities based on geographic accessibility in a 45-minute radius. New standards for licensing hospitals were also approved by the government.[27] Existing obsolete permission rules were replaced with a predictable regulation environment supportive of public heath. The number of business activities subject to licensing and permit regimes was reduced by 84%.[28]

Tender Requirements

Hospitals were expected to differ in size, with 15 to 25 beds in the Rayons[29] and over 100 more in regional centers and big cities. The minimum requirements were 50 square meters per bed in small hospitals and 75 square meters per bed in larger hospitals. These minimum requirements aimed to avoid excessive investments in hospital sector and to ensure cost stability of the privatized system.

Most importantly, the government did not aim to financially benefit from the privatization of the hospital sector. Investors took over existing hospitals in Tbilisi and the regional centers to create a minimum number of beds according to the tender conditions. Investors would then own the improved hospitals and were obliged to keep an agreed portfolio of medical services for no less than seven years. After meeting the obligations of the tender agreement, investors could utilize any unused property and the buildings of the old hospital for commercial purposes.

The War

The Russian–Georgian War of August 2008 necessitated significant changes in the privatization plans. The costs of the war and the subsequent economic downturn led many original investors to default. Most failed to find sufficient financial resources to build new hospitals in the ravaged country.

On investor in the New Hospital, Kakha Okriashvili, recalled these dark times, "In August, during the days of Russian military intervention, I asked a workman in a crane to keep working. I know that if we will stop working, it will show panic among all the families living near to hospital construction area."

New Hospital, a modern clinic with 450 beds in Tbilisi and a fashionable outpatient department, was one of the few projects that succeeded during the first stage of privatization. More than 20 million EUR had been invested by the private company PSP Georgia to rebuild the dilapidated former building of the Institute of Neurology and Eye Diseases.

The war's external shock, followed by a recession caused by contraction of foreign investment, made hospital privatization fail.

Restart of the Reforms

In April 2010, the hospital privatization process had been redesigned. The government changed the terms and conditions of state-funded health insurance.[30] The country outside of the capital was divided into 26 healthcare districts, and insurance companies were invited to compete for the opportunity to provide plans to the eligible poor for a period of three years in each of the districts. Insurers who expressed a willingness to participate in state insurance programs were obliged to renovate, build, and operate hospitals in their health districts.

By the end of 2013, up to 150 new hospitals of all sizes had been built and opened for operation, most of which was constructed through private investment from Georgia and other countries such as Austria, Canada, Israel, the Czech Republic, and the United Kingdom.

Reforming Health Financing

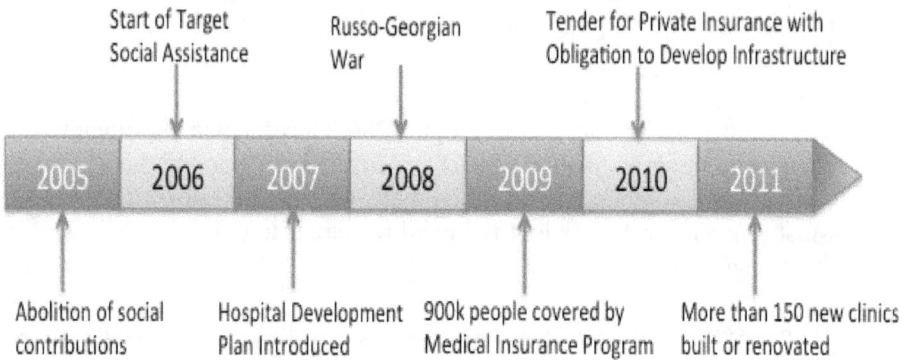

In the early 2000s, Georgia's health system was on the verge of collapse for the second time in ten years. In many cases, doctors have had to ask patients to bring their own medical supplies with them because they did not have sufficient funds to restock. The salaries of medical staff were frozen, including pensions and other social payments, because of economic stagnation and a growing budget deficit. According to data by the National Healthcare Association, Georgia's percentage of private spending as a share of total health expenditures grew from 84% to 88% from 2001 to 2003. As seen in the table below, central budget allocations as the percentage of total health spending decreased from 64% in 2002 to 49% in 2003. Private payment mechanisms were too weak to play any considerable role in the health system. The private insurance market remained undeveloped and did not contribute significantly to healthcare expenditures.

Mobilizing Resources

The termination of the social insurance tax was the first step in the chain of health funding reforms. The payroll tax covered less than 5% of total health expenditures, as healthcare was predominantly funded by out-of-pocket payments.

High unemployment and low wages, coupled with low tax rates, resulted in a thin revenue base, particularly since a large proportion of the population was involved in informal activities. These factors were catalyzed further by prevalent corruption in the public sector and a weak administrative capacity to enforce tax collection. Only five years after its introduction, the government saw no reason to continue the statutory social insurance and its payroll contributions.

In 2005, government contributions to medical insurance were removed altogether along with a general overhaul of the tax code. To improve its business climate and encourage investment, Georgia drastically reduced the number of taxes collected. Today, there are only six taxes, giving Georgia the fourth lowest tax burden in the world.

The government's success in combating corruption and encouraging economic growth quickly produced results. The stagnation in health financing and delays of public payments that plagued the country for years soon became history.

Starting in 2004, the government began dramatically increasing its health sector spending, though it remained low as a percentage of GDP compared to other developed countries. In 2003, public spending on health constituted just 0.6% of GDP. By 2010, the figure reached 1.8%. Total per capita health expenditure increased from 74 USD in 2003 to 256 USD in 2009.[31]

Healthcare Funding in Georgia 2001 and 2010	2001	2010
Share of total healthcare expenditure of GDP in %	7.8	10.2
Share of state healthcare expenditure of GDP in %	1.1	2.4
Share of private healthcare expenditures of the total health expenditures in %	76.7	74.0
Total annual healthcare expenditures per capita in USD	66$	270$

Health and Insurance Vouchers

On June 29, 2007, the Parliament of Georgia made more major reforms by introducing vouchers as an instrument to fund individual health services. Voucher-based financing substituted state purchasing as the primary instrument by which individuals access government-financed healthcare.

The health voucher was an earmarked account tied to each citizen to purchase entitled health services either online or in person. The law defined the main principles and characteristics of voucher-based financing as follows:

• Personalization.
Voucher beneficiaries can be a person or a group of persons such as a family.
• Freedom of choice.
Voucher beneficiaries have the right to choose a medical service supplier or insurance company
• Nondiscrimination
Voucher beneficiaries have the right to obtain medical insurance service without discrimination based on protected classes such as welfare, age, or health status.

Targeting the Poor

The defficiency of public funds and inefficiencies in administration rendered state health programs ineffective at achieving its main objective of securing patients from catastrophic healthcare costs. Due to widespread acceptance of illegal payments, poor families suffered much more than others that were better off.

In 2006, the government introduced a number of health financing reforms to reach the poor. First, a proxy means test was established to target public health subsidies for the neediest. Secondly, traditional supply-side subsidies that financed the public healthcare network were transformed into demand-side subsidies that lower individual insurance premiums for the vulnerable population. Thirdly, health service delivery was contracted out to the private sector in the spirit of privatization.

The first beneficiaries of free insurance vouchers were chosen based on welfare scores derived from the proxy means test. The development of target social assistance and monetization of social benefits was the product of social welfare reforms the Georgian government had introduced between 2004 and 2006.[32] Indeed, these reforms were part of a larger push to alleviate poverty through welfare reform called the Government Economic Development and Poverty Reduction Program.

In July 2007, the Georgian Prime Minister signed a decree setting conditions of insurance vouchers for citizens below the poverty line in Tbilisi and Imereti.[33] This decree served as a starting point for the government to improve financial access to health services and protect families under poverty line from health-related financial risks.

Under decree, more than 180,000 beneficiaries got state-funded health insurance vouchers with an overall budget of 17 million GEL.[34] The purpose of the pilot program was to test the appropriateness and administrative mechanisms of insurance coverage before launching the program across the country.

Any insurer with a license (with the exception of life insurers) could participate in these programs. In order to do so, an insurance company had to make an official statement that it would act in accordance with the government resolution.

The government resolution defined the entry procedure and responsibilities of insurance organizations to participate in the program. This was done to mitigate the common risks health systems experience in collaborating with for-profit insurance companies.

Equal Access Clause

Under Georgian law, insurance organizations have to ensure beneficiaries equal accessibility to insurance without any discrimination. It is prohibited for insurers to refuse issuing insurance to the beneficiary for any reason, to refuse prolonging an insurance contract for any reason, to terminate a policy during an contract term, and to refuse to fulfill its obligations.

Insurance organizations cannot add any additional premiums or other payments in the insurance contract period. Insurers are not allowed to provide policyholders with less conditions than those set by this decree, but are free to offer more.

Thanks to the reforms, formerly vague promises of government health programs were replaced with clearly defined regulations governing what is covered and what is not. To ensure fair funding, the insurance premium was calculated based on the recommendations of the Georgian Actuarial Association.

The number of beneficiaries covered by government-provided health insurance was almost 900,000 in 2010. Thanks to health reform in Georgia, access to essential healthcare services for vulnerable populations has significantly improved.

Improving Eligibility

From 2007 to 2011, state-funded health insurance coverage expanded to families of Internally Displaced Persons, public school teachers, policemen, and soldiers.

On September 1st, 2012, the government launched an extension of state-funded health insurance for an additional one million citizens — namely, retirees, university students, children under six, and under 18 with disabilities. Combined with the population that was already insured, the total share of Georgians covered by state-funded insurance accounted for 50% the population. The share of pre-paid services in healthcare grew from 5% to 45%.[35]

Developing Private Health Insurance

The development of state-funded insurance brought new challenges and opportunities to the Georgian insurance industry. Health insurance became the fastest growing line of business. Prior to 2006, private health insurance only played a marginal role in the healthcare system. Merely 40,000 Georgians had private health insurance, most of which were enrolled in group insurance policies.

In 2009, the so-called "Cheap 5 Lari Insurance" program was introduced and subsidized by the government for the population not covered by the state insurance program. The program aimed to "improve the financial accessibility of health services to Georgian citizens by increasing their enrollment in a voluntary health insurance."[36] It covered the costs of urgent care in the case of accidents, 50% of urgent non-accident inpatient care costs, urgent outpatient care, unlimited visits to a primary healthcare physician, and limited laboratory and diagnostic tests at the PHC level. Drugs were not included. The annual premium was 60 GEL[37], with two-thirds or 40 GEL funded by the government and one-third by the individual. Citizens and residents of Georgia between the ages of three and 65 were eligible to participate. The government expected that 300,000 to 500,000 people would sign up for the program. In reality, merely 122,000 people — 3% of population — purchased the insurance product. The program proved to be largely unappealing, mainly due to poor coverage and widespread distrust of the insurance industry. Fortunately, this proved to be a chance for private insurers to pilot individual insurance plans.

From 2009 to 2012, private health insurance became one of the most dynamic markets. Over that time period, insurance enrollment witnessed an increase of coverage from 40,000 to 450,000.

Share of the population with health insurance:

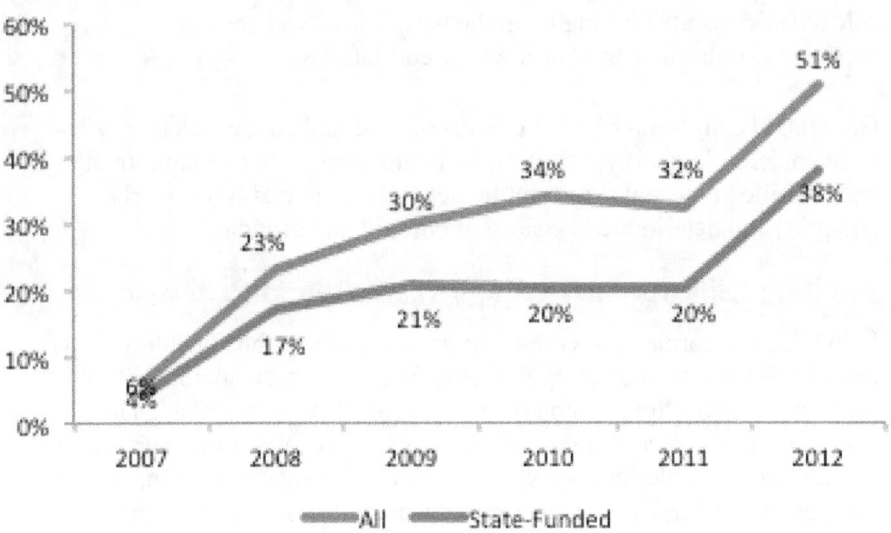

Consumer Protection: Mediation Services

The transfer of financing healthcare through private insurance required government regulators to monitor the performance of private insurance companies and ensure the protection of public interests.

A rapid switch from traditional state-administered social health programs to a private insurance model could have substantially increased the number of claim disputes. Given low insurance literacy among the population, many conflicts arose from confusion about policies' language. Moreover, brining these claims to court can be costly and time-consuming, particularly those below the poverty line. To address these issues, the government established a mediation service and call center to respond to customer questions beginning in May 2008.

In 2012, the mediation service (MMS) was established as a dispute resolution body by the Ministry of Labor, Health and Social Affairs.[38] The MMS hears disputes that originated after March 1st, 2012 between patients and insurance organizations, insurance organizations, and healthcare providers, as well as between patients and healthcare providers.

The disputes must relate to the provision of medical care, which is carried out through state and local budgets under the relevant healthcare programs. The MMS hears disputes upon the agreement of the parties. MMS decisions are binding upon the parties involved and can be appealed to court in accordance with Georgian law.

Georgia, like all former USSR countries, inherited an inefficient Soviet-style epidemiological system, troubled with corruption and unmotivated and unskilled personal. Most public health laboratories were poorly equipped and deteriorated because of chronic underfunding.

Fighting Corruption Through Institutional Redesign

In 2007, the Georgian government introduced new public health reforms to upgrade the Soviet sanitary model to 21st-century standards. In 2006, the State Sanitary Supervision Inspection (SSSI) was abolished. The SSSI was the most corrupt branch of the Ministry of Health, having been formally responsible for inspecting the sanitarian standards of markets and business enterprises. Its inspectors were notorious for collecting bribes from business owners.

After 2007, public health responsibilities have been delegated to municipalities, paid by earmarked transfers from the state budget. Under this arrangement, local public health institutions are still managed by municipal governments, while major public health functions such as inspections are paid for by the central government. It is worth mentioning that among post-Soviet countries, only Georgia has taken up this model; all others have retained the bureaucratic system of the USSR without major organizational changes.[39]

Reforming Georgian Pharmaceutical Market

In Georgia, access to medication is far from universal. The ability to pay for drugs is one of the most common problems reported by Georgian households. Nevertheless, pharmaceutical companies greatly benefited from the market-oriented reforms. The Georgian pharmaceutical market grew dramatically, from approximately 57 million USD in 2001 to 245 million USD in 2011.

The growth of the pharmaceutical industry was accompanied by a steep increase in households' pharmaceutical expenditures. The share of household income spent on pharmaceuticals is higher in Georgia than in most develop countries. Household spending increased by 85% per capita, rising from 105 to 194 GEL from 2007 to 2010.[40] The purchase of medical goods accounted for 60% of the total healthcare expenditures per household in 2010. This amount is four times higher than the average rate among most OECD countries, which is about 15%.[41] Georgia currently spends 4% of its GDP on pharmaceuticals. This fraction is double that of the US, a country known for its high expenditures on pharmaceuticals. Furthermore, retail per capita consumption of pharmaceuticals in Georgia is quite low, at 35 USD per year, compared to 62 USD in Ukraine, 99 USD in Russia, and a range of 200 to 400 USD in Europe.[42]

According to a 2010 study conducted by the Curatio International Foundation on the availability and affordability of pharmaceuticals in Georgia, brand name drugs were typically more expensive in the country than in the EU, usually by a wide margin. At the same time, most generic drugs were cheaper in Georgia than the rest of the EU.

A few companies' market dominance led to high markups for medicine, which explain the high prices and expenditures for pharmaceuticals. A number of additional factors contributed to the problems in pharmaceutical market, including high levels of self-treatment, and doctors receiving financial incentives from large pharmaceutical companies to overprescribe.

Liberalization of the Drug Market

In November 2009, the government began taking proactive measures to address the issue of unaffordable pharmaceutical prices. Amendments to the Law on Drugs and Pharmaceutical Regulation were introduced to increase competition in the market and expand import opportunities for companies by removing trade barriers.

The new pharmaceutical policy had three main objectives. First, to ease the import of drugs on approved lists in other industrialized countries. Second, to make it easier for new market actors to import drugs directly to hospitals, doctors, and insurers. Third, to loosen regulations regarding retail pharmacy space so as to allow supermarkets and others venders to sell medicine.

Import opportunities were also expanded through the so-called "recognition policy" and by allowing parallel imports of pharmaceuticals. Complex and overly bureaucratic registration procedures were simplified by introducing automatic registration for products recognized by the European Medicine Agency (EMA), the United States' Food and Drugs Administration (FDA), and other internationally recognized pharmaceutical regulatory bodies. These new import opportunities also made it possible for existing importers to ship medicine directly from the European market, where they are often cheaper than Georgia and CIS countries.

Since the beginning of 2011, the Georgian Parliament banned doctors from prescribing drugs on ready letterheads and recommending specific products to patients of pharmaceutical companies. For the first violation of the norms the doctor is waiting for a fine of 571 dollars, for the second - the amount is doubled.

In April 2010, new outpatient drug benefits were added to the Medical Insurance Program for the Poor. Program enrollees were allowed to purchase approved essential drugs with 50% co-payment by the Ministry of Health and an annual limit of 50 GEL. In 2012, the annual limit rose to 200 GEL for the state insurance program for pensioners.

Competition Reduced Pharmacies Margins

As a result of the new market-oriented reforms, pharmaceutical prices started to decline in 2009 for the first time in the post-Soviet era. In 2012, the Curatio International Foundation published comprehensive statistical research about pharmaceutical markups between 2009 and 2011 and discovered that the average prices dropped by 30%. Price reductions were most profound for original brands in the PSP/Aversi/ GPC network, a major player in the market, because of increased competition.

According to study's main findings, market competition dropped the markup of original brands by 75% through 2012. Mark-up reductions for OBs were most dramatic within PSP/Aversi/GPC (from 90.7% to 21.5%) than other competing pharmacy networks.

As a result, the cost of receiving pharmaceutical treatment has declined drastically over the last four years. In 2012, the standard price of treatment was 50%-60% less than 2009.[43]

Granted, the prices and availability of prescribed medicines is still a problem for most Georgians, and further efforts to enhance free competition and quality of care are needed. However, the initial results have been promising.

Results of the Reforms

Health reform lead to huge improvements of Georgians' well-being and transformed citizens' medical spending to one of the lowest levels in Europe.

In 2011, Georgians' life expectancy at birth rate exceeded that of the CIS countries and is close to the indicator of the European region according to the WHO data. Today, Georgians can expect to live 74.5 years, compared to 71 in 2000.[44]

According to the National Statistics Service, the main source of mortality data in Georgia, under 5 mortality has been declining since 2003.[45]

Under-five mortality rates per 1 000 live births, Georgia, 2000-2011:

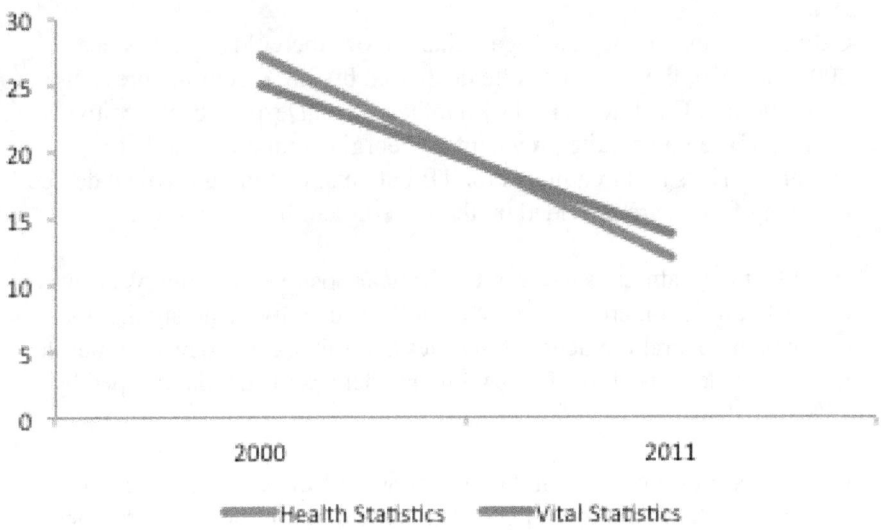

Since 2003, Georgia has experience a decline of the infant mortality rate. According to the survey data, the average infant mortality rate decreased by 66.1% from 1995 to 2009.

Since 2003, the maternal mortality rate has also declined. One comprehensive maternal mortality study was conducted in 2011 that tracked all hospital deaths of women aged 15–49 in 2010. The results were close to official statistics.

Preventive immunization coverage is close to the level of coverage seen in EU. In 2011, it was 91%.

The proportion of births attended by skilled medical personnel reached its highest point of 99.8% in 2011. Antenatal and postnatal care is one of the central components of Georgia's child health system. Since 2000, coverage with 4 complete antenatal visits has been increasing and it exceeded the WHO global indicator.

Georgia has a low prevalence HIV at below 0.01% of the population. Significant progress has been made in preventative treatment. The Joint United Nations Program on HIV/AIDS recognizes Georgia as a country that provides universal access to Anti-Retroviral Therapy. Despite wide availability of treatment, Georgia still has one of the highest rates of AIDS in Europe at 4.1 in 100,000 people, compared to an average of 1.5 in Eastern Europe as a whole.

Georgia has experienced a huge reduction of tuberculosis (TB) since 2009. In 2010, the incidence rate decreased by 2.8% from the previous year, and in 2011 it decreased by another 4.5%. Despite these positive results, TB remains quite prevalent in Georgia compared to other countries. Tests and treatments for TB patients, including medical device reporting forms, are provided by the government free of charge.

In 2005, the treatment success rate of smear positive pulmonary TB was 64%. By 2011, it increased to 76%. In 2011, there were no significant changes in general incidents of measles and rubella. Incidence of measles in children decreased by 17.4% while incidences of rubella dropped by 73%.

Other countries, both rich and poor, can learn from Georgia's health reforms to rethink the role of government and public-private partnerships in the health sector.

Chapter 3: Georgia's Health Reform's in a European Context

By Michael Tanner, Cato Institute

If rising pension costs are the biggest threat to the modern welfare state, the rising cost of healthcare is a close second. This seems particularly ironic since so many American commentators have called for the United States to adopt a European model for delivering healthcare. Indeed, it can be argued that the US's latest effort at healthcare reform, the Patient Protection and Affordable Care Act, remakes much of our healthcare system in a European manner.

Yet, Europe clearly has not solved the conundrum of trying to expand access while controlling costs. Although every European country spends less on healthcare than the US, the cost of care is nonetheless rising faster in nearly all EU countries than the level of funding available to pay for them. As the *Wall Street Journal* notes, "Europeans…face steeper medical bills in the future in their cash-strapped governments." At the same time, European efforts at cost control have frequently resulted in direct or indirect rationing that makes their nations promises of universal coverage ring increasingly hollow.

Facing the worst of both worlds — rising costs *and* rationed access — many European countries have begun to introduce market mechanisms into their systems. Thus, while the US has shifted toward more of a European-style health system over the past few years, Europe is shifting toward a system that looks more like the US. But, such reforms have been tentative to date, and many may well end up being too little, too late.

The International Monetary Fund estimates that on average, healthcare spending by European governments will increase by two percentage points of GDP by 2030 and more than 3 percentage points of GDP in Austria, Great Britain, Greece, Iceland, Luxembourg, Portugal, and Switzerland. While that might not seem a great deal at first glance, it is extremely significant when one considers how high government spending as a percent of GDP already is in those countries. European countries simply don't have the leeway to absorb the increase. Looking further out in the future, the increase grows worse. By 2050, the average increase is expected to exceed 6.5 percent of GDP. That alone would drive government spending in the average EU country to more than 59% of GDP.

While the relationship between age and health expenditures is not simple, the body of evidence suggests that the elderly are increasingly consuming intensive healthcare. Europeans aged 65 and over account for as much as 40 percent of healthcare spending in the EU — far more than any other demographic group. Longer life expectancies do not necessarily translate directly into more years of healthy life. In fact, healthy life expectancy, defined as the number of years that a person can expect to live without having a major disease or injury, is generally 7 to 10 years less than life expectancy itself.

For example, by some estimates, chronic diseases account for as much as 70% of healthcare costs. The elderly are more likely to have at least one chronic disease, if for no other reason than the fact that a longer lifespan provides more time for a body's natural genetic breakdown to occur. Already, nearly one-third of Europe's population has a chronic disease or condition. As the number of senior citizens rises, so too will the cost of caring for them.

When patients do not directly bear the cost of their healthcare consumption, they have an incentive to over-consume. When a demand unconstrained by price meets a finite supply of healthcare goods and services, it is a recipe for obvious problems.

Rationing

While fighting a losing battle against rising healthcare costs, many European countries have attempted to control expenditures by limiting the availability of certain drugs and technologies or by restricting access to various providers and procedures. In other words, they have restored to rationing.

Although Americans tend to recoil at any hint of rationing, it is important to understand that it is not intrinsically bad, and, indeed, is inevitable in some form. Healthcare is a commodity — and a finite one at that. There are only so many doctors, hospitals, and, most importantly, money to go around. Yet, at the same time, no one wants to die. If a treatment can save lives or increase quality of life, people generally want it. After all, in the long run, the only way to spend less on healthcare is to consume less of it. Someone has to say "no."

Georgia's Reforms

Georgia's health system before the Rose Revolution was a centralized system almost completely controlled and planned by the government. It strove to provide comprehensive, free, and accessible care for everyone. Despite these stated intentions, the system was drastically underfunded, the healthcare it provided was inadequate, and access to care was far from universal. While the centralized system had some success in the control of communicable diseases, it was insufficiently flexible to keep pace with evolving healthcare needs.

In the post-Soviet period, the Georgian system had been stuck in a mix of centralized, state-funded healthcare with a small degree of privatization for citizens who could afford better care. The collapse of the Soviet Union and the centrally planned economic system with it left a large proportion of Georgians in poverty. Incremental steps to reform the health system had seen costs continue to rise while doing little to improve healthcare outcomes. As a result, many Georgians continued to suffer.

Widespread dissatisfaction with the slow progress of the post-Soviet period ushered in the Rose Revolution and a new government focused on reorienting the Georgian economy and faltering healthcare system towards the free market. Mandatory social health insurance, introduced in the 1990's and plagued by inefficiency, was abolished. State health facilities were privatized, and health workers were no longer government employees.

In keeping with the broader reforms of the Rose Revolution, which placed a strong belief in the free market, the regulatory role of the state in healthcare has been greatly diminished. Instead, the focus shifted to allowing market mechanisms to regulate the system in the hope that the most necessary and efficient regulations would evolve through the interactions between individuals, providers, and public authorities.

The reforms have been effective in keeping healthcare costs down, especially compared to the growth in health spending in the developed countries of Europe and the US. Total health expenditure only increased as a percentage of GDP from 8.5% in 2003 to only 9.9% in 2011. The effects of the recession explain much of this increase, as total health expenditures jumped from 9% of GDP in 2008 to 10.2 percent in 2009. Since this initial spike, they have actually declined, returning to levels below 10 percent of GDP.

Meanwhile, the government share of health expenditures has remained relatively steady over the same period. While this is a higher amount than many of its neighbors, it reflects both Georgia's faster economic growth than other former CIS countries and the fact that that the country does not rely on centralized cost controls to keep healthcare spending down.

The proportion of the population living below the national poverty line was above 24% in 2009, in part because of the global recession, and in part due to the lingering effects of transitioning away from the Soviet economy. By international standards defining poverty as those living on less than $1.25 a day (adjusted for purchasing power parity), the poverty rate was roughly 15% in 2009. Georgia has devised a way to provide targeted assistance to people who would otherwise face adverse health outcomes due to lack of care while, at the same time, minimizing market distortions and bolstering its fledgling insurance industry. Since 2008, Georgians living below the poverty line have been provided with vouchers to purchase private health insurance plans. Through this mechanism, as opposed to a state health insurance scheme, Georgia places the decision-making power in the hands of individual consumers and encourages competition among insurance providers. Consumers are not insulated from the costs of healthcare, and providers compete for lower costs and improve quality in order to attract customers.

Georgians not living below the poverty line are expected to purchase their own private health insurance voluntarily or pay out of pocket for services. The very targeted and limited government intervention in healthcare, restricted to those below the poverty line, has allowed the Georgian health system to suffer from far less market distortion than most developed countries in Europe and the US.

While the healthcare system has markedly improved over the system in place prior to the Rose Revolution, there remains some room for improvement. Out-of-pocket payments still comprise a large proportion of health expenditures, and these people not covered by prepaid private health insurance are susceptible to catastrophic healthcare costs. The path forward for Georgia is for out-of-pocket payments to be formalized and a sizable portion to be transferred to pre-paid private schemes, thereby reducing the share of out-of-pocket payments in total health expenditures. A greater reliance on private health insurance would improve protection against catastrophic healthcare costs, and the health outcomes for the country's citizenry would improve. While seeking to promote the role of the private insurance industry, the Georgian government must resist the temptation to expand its regulatory role and introduce additional market distortions that could derail its emerging health insurance industry. Progress is being made already, and the insurance system is starting to take hold as the number of insured people has reached 1.5 million, more than a third of the population.

Georgia's focus on free-market mechanisms to reshape it healthcare system can serve as a framework to other former CIS countries in the region, whose more centralized systems have struggled to keep pace. While there are doubtlessly more areas to improve, such as decreasing reliance on out-of-pocket payments and growing the role of the private health insurance industry, the Georgian healthcare system that has emerged from the Rose Revolution has managed to improve healthcare outcomes, rein in the growth of healthcare costs, and given the system the flexibility it needs to the changing healthcare needs of an aging demography. While there is still work to be done, the free market innovations in Georgia's healthcare system have resulted in marked improvements and, in many ways, can serve as a template for other countries in the region.

A Model for Reform?

Europe's welfare states are learning a simple but important lesson that there is no such thing as free healthcare. In fact, not only is healthcare not free, the rapidly rising cost of European healthcare is adding enormously to their budget woes.

As a result, most European countries have begun inching toward reform, removing some price controls and requiring patients to pay a larger proportion of their healthcare bills. But, for the most part, while such reforms have created an unmistakable trend toward freer markets in healthcare, they have so far been little more than baby steps. They may be too little, too late to avoid further rationing and continued budgetary pressures.

Georgia, on the other hand, has been much more aggressive about implementing market-based healthcare reform. It is, of course, far too early to determine the success of such reforms, but the initial results are promising. If such trends continue, Georgia could end up as a model for European health reform.

Bendukidze, Roeder, Tanner, Urushadze

44

Chapter 4: An Interview with Kakha Bendukidze, Former Georgian Minister for Reform Coordination

"I understood that this is the crucial moment. If I can kill this idea, then we have a chance to go to a private system."

Q: So, initially I would be interested in what you see as the most important steps of the Georgian health reforms. If you could point out the main steps which, in your opinion, were crucial for setting up the right institutions.

KB: I think liberalizing the system by allowing that the private providers and private insurance were very important steps in order to get rid of the single payer and single provider system.

The question is what is the product of health care. Health care is mainly selling a service of getting healthy. You become ill, you go to the doctor, and have the services provided to you. But this understanding is deeply wrong. It's not the service which healthcare is selling. Healthcare is selling being healthy service. So, I read many years ago how healthcare was organized in Ancient Chinese villages. They have a doctor, and this doctor was paid one egg or chicken by each family when each family member was healthy. When something goes wrong, they stop paying. So the doctor was motivated not to spend money for healing but to spend money for preventing disease. This the product. You should organize the system that way. The system as a whole is setting the product of maintaining health.

It's a three-pillar system. You have patient, you have provider, and you have insurer. The patient by definition is a private person. You have private hospitals and state funding, state single account, state company.

It's an unavoidable the collusion of two private parties to cheat non-private parties. If you have private insurance companies, private patients and state healthcare providers, it's an unavoidable collusion of two private parties against the state party. It will happen, and there is a way to control it but it is quite expensive. So, it's important to have all three parts private. If they are competing for the resources, they are exchanging information based on their own interests, which is only natural, and their balancing the information asymmetry by having their own private interests. That's the most important thing.

In Georgia it was very simple because the system was totally rotten. We had many several hundred providers, 98% of them state-owned, and we had 100% a state-funded universal healthcare system. The results were completely insufficient and nobody was happy.

The funny thing is the Georgian population was sure that there is no universal coverage. Nobody believed that there was actually a universal health system. The problem was in that system it was uncertain what will happen. It was preventing the development of private sector. The few private hospitals we had were not very competitive. They were a little bit better, they provide better care, but the infrastructure was underdeveloped because nobody wanted to invest. This universal coverage was not working and the actual coverage in the universal coverage was below 25% of cases, so usually state funding comes on a monthly basis. That caused that one week per month a procedure was covered and three weeks a month they were taking money for the same procedure. This was actually legal.

Q: Did doctors and nurses also ask for bribes?

KB: Often doctors were taking money, the nurses were taking money, etc. This is how the universal coverage would work: **Because this is a system that happens quite frequently when you want to have some good social justice things you want to fight poverty. The result is not fighting poverty but fighting poor people and helping rich people.**

Imagine you have limited amount of funds in capital city and you know that you cannot use these funds for everyone. So, you are chief operating officer or CEO of hospital, so what will be your decision: For whom to use these funds? The political situation and setup of social networks give you an answer: you should use these funds for VIPs. Because, first of all before you have universal coverage and some Member of Parliament comes to your hospital. Why should you take money from him? He will be unhappy, he maybe knows that there is universal coverage, he will say it's illegal … you want him to be happy, and also you will use this money maybe for some really loud cases. So this is how it was working. And in reality it was maintaining huge political power of these guys in the system. So, the Minister of Healthcare was a very important political player and the chief doctors, the heads of hospitals were very important because this just helped you solve medical problem – free of charge.

This was also bred with a lot of overregulation, which has nothing to do with quality. I can tell you several anecdotes — it sounds like a joke.

Q: That would be great.

KB: So, first of all, how I get involved in healthcare reform: First year I was serving Minister for Economy and in the second year, I was Minister for Reforms Coordination with very small office but a quite wide scope of work and a wide mandate. In early 2005 we were dealing with licensing system in general and I was holding meetings with different ministries, discussing what their licensing looks like and how it's done, and we want to make a unified licensing law which will cover all legal ways of how things will be licensed like the one-stop-shop. We also aimed to cut the number of licenses. **In 2005 we had exactly 1,024 licenses in healthcare.**

Q: In healthcare?

KB: Yeah. Including some like license to perform kidney surgery for kids was another, like license to perform kidney surgery for adults was separate. These licenses were granted to the hospitals, and we have several funny licenses like using 'cosmic waves', like traditional medicine, something very weird.

We were discussing at least consolidating licenses and there was opposition from the Minister of Healthcare. And at this moment my sister calls me and says, "We have problem with a mother something with heart and she's hospitalized in that hospital." And it was a private hospital near the house where she was living. I spent my life outside Georgia, so I don't know the infrastructure well. So, I told these people I'll go to my mother for maybe like 40 minutes, please go take some coffee and I'll be back, because it's part of the parliamentary hearing in two weeks. I go to see my mom and I ask my driver, do you know where this is? He says, "yeah yeah yeah, I know", and after twenty minutes we are moving through some piles of trash, and I tell him okay you don't know direction ask someone. And he says, "No, no, no, that's the direction." And we stopped between several piles of trash and that's the hospital. It was an ugly, half demolished building. I saw my sister looking from the building. She says, "Come to fourth floor." There was a strange elevator and it was more or less clean there. Everything was ok with my mother.

When I went back to my office, I tell these people at the ministry, "Are you crazy? Which positive regulations are you talking about?" Because when I was going to hospital, I thought this would be some nice green garden and there would be small building in this garden and it would be clean and nice services, and instead of it I saw this building. The bureaucrats told me "Yeah, yeah, this system of license isn't working properly." And I said, "Okay, if it's not working properly, it should be abolished." But not to cause a lot of problems, just let consolidate and reduce the licenses to 57 in total.

That was how I entered healthcare and I understood that this system cannot fix itself. One of the problems was that this system was completely managed by doctors, and I made some research in European countries on who are the ministers of healthcare and I found in half of the cases there was nonmedical staff. I went to the Prime Minister and said, "Look, we need to do something because this guys (Ministers of Health) will never change the situation because they can do very good, they are very progressive, but they are thinking in terms of not only how they would teach the Semashko system, but they also have a problem with dealing with other people. Because he was his schoolmate he was his classmate, he was his student, he was his professor, so they're all connected. I had a Deputy Minister of Healthcare working closely with me and we did lots of work together but he knows everyone because he was professor of medical university and he has lots of students and if doctor was young he was his student if doctor was old he was his teacher.

And because the idea of having private providers was weird at that moment. So, I was talking a lot with Minister of Health, how to privatize, maybe like giving ownership to medical personnel, but to **privatize, privatize, privatize.**

Also the Minister had Andria Urushadze as an advisor, who became Minister of Health some years later. He was supportive of the idea of privatizing, but he was not sure and scared of what would happen. And what helped me, there was World Bank research on how to reform Georgian healthcare. Of course their findings were nothing special. And it was a design based on calculations, which were not wrong, and the result was in Georgia we should have only three hospitals. And totally, we need 3,600 modern beds so we can have several hospitals. They set the locations of these hospitals, and the World Bank was ready to fund this. We have a government meeting discussing that at crazy length. I was sure that it cannot work.

First of all, we'll build these hospitals but nobody would close the old hospitals. And also, when I talk with Ministry of Healthcare officials, they were saying, "Okay, they will die by themselves."

I understood that this is the crucial moment. If I can kill this idea, then we have a chance to go to a private system. And I tell the government, I think the most important argument is in the Semashko system in each region, and in Georgia we have more than sixty region, we have at least one hospital. Everyone knows that there's a hospital in their city. So, what's our political message? Forget that your local hospital. Now you need to go to another city 150 kilometers from here to get hospital services. And the government's reaction to this scenario was that it's politically unacceptable. We cannot declare that you will not have local hospitals.

I said, "That means that we need to have some ready plan how to reform these hospitals." And everyone understands that we have 60, 70, or 200 small hospitals scattered around the city, you cannot centrally manage those. So, the only way is to privatize it.

And I remember the Prime Minister asked the Minister of Healthcare: "Oh, can you tell us, is there real private hospitals existing anyplace in world?" And he said, "Yeah for example Mayo Clinic is private hospital." So, that was the big achievement. After we designed the plan, which was called The Hospital Sector Reform General Master Plan, I agreed with the World Bank estimation that we need not more than 3,000 something beds. Officially Georgia had 12,000 beds

Yeah, they were underutilized. Big empty building, there is no patients and just some physical beds.

Also it was clear that the patients are one-fourth in capital city and three-fourths outside of the capitol. But, you cannot design a system that way. You can have what's called community hospital, and the idea was not let's design a plan which will be part of this **public-private partnership idea, and the private sector should build, operate, and own these hospitals**. Maybe we will have some excess of beds, but not huge excess. We designed a plan to reduce the amount of beds by 50 percent.

It was not very radical. And the plan allocated 90% of beds to capital city and several big cities, and only 10% of the beds to the community hospitals. **At the same time we the problem that there was a completely undeveloped health insurance market in Georgia.**

Due to the marginal role of private insurance markets in Georgia, we knew that private healthcare insurance would not achieve very high performance for several years. The idea was that we have private providers and private insurance companies. In order to cover the poor in such a system we moved from a universal coverage to means-based coverage by providing healthcare voucher to people below the poverty line. The plan was that this covers half of the population with vouchers from government and them using the vouchers for purchasing.

Q: So, one question regarding the privatization of the hospitals. Am I right that you basically gave the hospitals away under the conditions that the new owners invest in them? You didn't sell them, but you basically gave them away.

KB: Yeah, political constraint which was articulated by the Prime Minister. We cannot, at that moment, privatize hospitals for cash because that will mean government was making money on people's healthcare. In other words, historically hospitals in the biggest part of hospitals in Tbilisi, they were located in the old part of city where the real estate price was really high. And they were not reflected the real distribution of patients in the city. They were small and not very effective buildings. In a way, these buildings would not work properly. Some of them were built 150 years ago. The idea was let's set a conditional competitive process.

So, you get this hospital, which is centrally located, not very functional, but maybe, a highly valued real estate. Instead of maintaining the dysfunctional hospital in the old town we made contracts with the new owners that allowed them to sell the highly valued real estate when guaranteeing that they will build a new hospital in Tbilisi and build several community hospitals in the Rayons.

So the idea was that you will have several hospital chains, and there are several big hospitals and several satellite hospitals. They will have their own referral system. The process of privatization coincided with the global financial crisis and the war with Russia.

Today Georgia is a country where private providers provide the majority of beds. We have several state-owned hospitals. I think the current government will increase the number of state-owned beds, but in general the system is at least mixed with dominance of private hospitals, and I think that there is healthy competition in the system.

Q: One technical question regarding these packages or bundles of hospitals: Was it the Ministry of Health or Economics basically bundled hospitals with another? And were same Investors able or allowed to buy a number of packages or bundles?

KB: It was I working with Minister of Healthcare and investors were able to obtain various bundles in a competitive process. First of all, there will be sort of creative destruction even within the bundles. You may have, several twenty-bed hospitals in the region. Some chains will transform the regional outlets to ambulances and focus on well-developed day care in the Regions and move for the surgery to the hospital chain's main hospital. This sort of portfolio consolidation happens on the market.

Second, new investors will come and invest. Because they will understand that this is a country with a private healthcare system, and it happens, there is significant construction of private hospitals in Georgia. About 1,000 new beds have been constructed since the privatization. Some Azeri businessman from Baku came to Tbilisi and saw the opportunity to invest in the hospital sector. His 250-bed private hospital is under construction near to my University.

Of course, the main backbone of system, are still the brownfield investment that were given away with the bundles but also smaller greenfield investments can be seen in the Georgian healthcare market. In each regional center, there is more than one small community hospital, and this system is working that way. Of course, the initial idea was based on complete competition in every way. The government is providing vouchers to people below some level of poverty and those people are choosing which insurance company they want to be covered by. And then the respective insurance company deals with hospital how they want that patient to be serviced.

Q: The healthcare service pricing just happens on the market, right?

KB: Yeah, we're just providing the voucher that is adjusted to market-based estimation of what is the premium. This also depends on whom you are providing insurance.

Q: So, I think that's very comprehensive regarding privatization. I think what would be most interesting for readers from other post-soviet countries is how you successfully managed to crush the resistance of doctors. How you basically took health policy away from doctors.

KB: That was the biggest challenge, as I explained, and the good thing was that the system was completely discredited. Nobody believed that it will work as it is. Also, many doctors found that they can be successful in this new system because they can deal with investors, they can help investors in the health system. **Also, we added some sweeteners**: In healthcare you have some key persons. Let's say professors in charge of some whatever-ology. Most of them they were heading some dysfunctional former existing healthcare institution. We offered them some small premises that they can privatize cheaply like 100 dollar per square meter. And then they can build their own, small, private whatever they want and that premises. And that was one of this part of plan and the doctors were happy because they got their own clinics.

Q: I think that's very valuable. Probably we should move on to the liberalization of the pharmaceutical market.

KB: It was very clear that we need to open the pharmaceutical market, but it takes several years to do what was clear in the beginning. **It took four steps in order to open the pharmaceutical market.**

The initial part took place when we were dealing with the licensing issue. So, I found that there were complicated licenses in permit issue to open a drug store, you need a special permit, a general license and there was first, second, and third type of drug store. The first class of drug store which can sell anything needs hundred forty square meters of premises, two independent entrances. Also, there was restriction that you cannot have a drug store within the hospital building. Also, you had licensing for pharmaceutical import. Hospitals were surrounded by drug stores because everyone want to build them there.

We canceled the licensing of import. For testability, wholesalers just have to inform the Ministry that they have purchased a certain drug. At that moment Georgia had three pharmaceutical chains, two big and one smaller. These chains they were running pharmacies, they had some blistering activities, and they were the main importers of drugs. And also there was a system of registration of any pharmaceutical like in any country, it was five-year registration. It cost not a lot compared to other countries, compared to former Soviet countries, it was $2,000 or something like that.

The registration of drugs in Georgia dis-incentivized many large drug manufacturers to enter the Georgian market. Imagine you are a large pharmaceutical company and you want to register a drug in a small country like Georgia. They know that registering drugs in small developing countries is often combined with bribes. That's why big pharmaceutical companies gave exclusive distribution licenses to Georgian wholesalers and pharmacy chains. This registration hurdle created leverage for importers due to the exclusivity they are granted with. That kept prices quite high.

We needed to first simplify how pharmacies are working and allow also selling pharmaceuticals in regular shops. Second, it's clear that we need to dis-bundle this registration issue. Aspirin was invented close to 100 years ago and nothing will happen in terms of safety or unexpected effects. **But what the hell we need to register once in five years Aspiring in Georgia? What good are we creating that way? What could happen with Aspirin?**

It was clear that if you have drugs that were produced in countries like Germany or Switzerland und they are approved in those countries the drugs can also be used in Georgia without additional registration.

Also we liberalized drugs' imports completely and allowed parallel imports. So, what were the consequences? First, most of the big pharmaceutical companies established warehouses in Georgia. You can sell your drugs to some big hospital. You cut out the unneeded middleman from the chain.

We got two additional pharmacy chains in Georgia. So, now there are five. The market shares of these chains are less than they were before. The first reduction of the market share of big chains was first happening in 2005 when we reduced the requirements of how to start a pharmacy. So, it was the first boost of small pharmacies around the country. **The**

prices for most of the drugs went down, but the most interesting and funny thing is that the profits of pharmaceutical companies went up.

Because allowing the parallel import created leverage for importers to talk with producers about prices. Importers can now purchase drugs from markets where drugs are sold very cheap (e.g. Greece). That reduced purchasing expenses of importers Georgia.

In some countries, there are government subsidies for drugs, they go sometimes directly to the wholesaler. There was big resistance by Georgian pharmacy chains. They were opposing the reforms. After we liberalized parallel imports and abolished registration rules it took about eight months for the market to adjust and to provide consumers with cheaper drugs at the same quality.

Q: So, I think we can come to your current assessment of what happened to the health system since fall 2012 and what your current outlook is. Will the market-based character of the Georgian health system prevail?

KB: Of course, nothing lasts forever. Only the pyramids, maybe. From October 2012 on we have new government, a very populist government. And he first Prime Minister of that government appointed a Minister of Health who was running the heavily funded hospital in the Prime Minister's hometown. This state-owned hospital is fully funded by the former Prime Minister. Fully-funded based on worse case Semashko system. So, let's say that average stay of patients which in European countries was four days, in Georgia was five days – in this hospital it was thirty-days. Because, who cares, you have unlimited funding, you have newly refurbished hospital, you can stay there one month. It is good for the doctor because nothing bad happens to patient, and it's good for patient because he comes from a remote village and is now sitting in a good and modern environment.

So the former head of this hospital is now Minister of Healthcare. He's more aggressive than other ministers trying to demolish the system. The direction is more or less clear so they want to make the system much more regulated including regulation of costs, which is impossible actually, but he thinks that he can regulate costs in each hospital. They want to go to universal coverage, they declared it, but there is not enough money for universal coverage, and they (the state) want to run some hospitals, which I think they will.

But, the good part of the story is there is not enough funding for universal healthcare. So, reality is that there is no universal healthcare. At the same time, you have private providers, some of them quiet big. You have private insurance companies who have knowledge of private insurance, and these insurance companies are trying to provide the tiny part that is covered by pseudo-universal insurance and the additional coverage that they are selling, supplementary insurance. Supplementary insurance is much bigger than the basic benefit package defined by the new government.

Q: Okay, so the universal coverage is already introduced?

KB: Yeah, it's introduced, but it's not universal. There was something called "universal coverage," but is not universal coverage because there is no money for universal coverage. Universal coverage is maybe 40% of needs - so 60% are out-of-pocket or healthcare insurance payments depending on how effective health insurance is. The current government also wants to tighten regulation in the pharmaceutical market. It looks like we will have some sort of compromise.

So, the important part of the story is that the means-tested system is very unpopular. It takes huge political will to consider means-tested system because when you have a loud minority which is close to means-tested part and a little bit above and they are unhappy because they are not receiving this aid. In Georgia the system was completely dysfunctional – This helped us to introduce a totally new and private system.

Of course, there were mistakes also. For example, government in 2009 decided to equip the insurance companies with temporary regional monopolies and thus taking the freedom of choice away from the patients. There is nothing bad with in monopolies as long as monopolies are based on market forces. But Government is the creator of bad monopolies.

Another question is that, big question that people raise, is the system of private greed-based insurance companies better for providing services which are funded by government because they are caring about profit. It's not clear that single big government insurance company can do the same with less money. Of course, if you go to some simplistic modeling and find that you can have ten insurance companies and merge them in one and also tell them that you don't care about profit, you can significantly reduce overhead and significantly reduce cost.

But that's the price that we are paying for stability of the system or competitiveness of the system. When you have just a single insurance you don't have a benchmark.

But not only we have new hospitals but we have completely new insurance companies arising coming from countries such as Austria and Israel. And was it very successful? No. You also have creative destruction because one insurance company went bankrupt. Because this insurance company was ineffective. And, also what happens with this private providers: Actually some of them look really successful. They merge and acquire other private providers, so the largest private provider today in Georgia has something like 1,200 beds all over Georgia, so it's a real network and an insurance company owns them, so they're providing integrated services. The situation is competitive and they're looking to have an IPO in London this year.

I think that's a very good story. It was based on marketing which can rise capital, because that was one of the questions: How can the system develop when it's private using this sort of funding using the market, which is not available when healthcare is state-funded. Also, it's clear that when you have several big providers chains of hospitals you can realize efficiencies.

There are lots of legends in healthcare and the biggest are that it is not a market, it's not price-sensitive, the market laws are not working there, it's a responsibility of government to provide everything, etc.

In reality, we know that if a service shall be produced in an effective manner, it should go to someone who conducts lots of it. And I hope in Georgia we have some healthy foundation for the private providers. If government will not do really crazy things, the private hospital sector will continue to develop.

About the Authors:

Andria Urushadze: Urushadze served as the Minister of Health, Labour and Social Affairs of Georgia from September 10, 2010 to March 15, 2012. He was born on April 25, 1968 in Tbilisi, Georgia. In 1993, he graduated from the General Medicine Department of Tbilisi State Medical University. In 1993-1994, he took post graduate courses in Endocrinology at the same institution. In 1997, he completed studies at the School of Governance. He then completed Special Training Course for Executive Managers of Insurance Companies in Switzerland in 1998. From 1993 through 1995, he was the Vice-President of Georgian Youth International Foundation. In 1995-1997, Urushadze was the head of the International Programs Implementation Bureau at the State Chancellery of Georgia. From 1997 until 2005, he was the Executive Director of an insurance company.

Kakha Bendukidze: Bendukidze is a Georgian politician and businessman. After the Rose Revolution, he served as Georgian Minister of Economy (June–December 2004), Minister for Reform Coordination (December 2004 - January 2008) and Head of the Chancellery of Government of Georgia (February 2008 - February 2009). Bendukidze graduated from the Department of Biology of Tbilisi State University in 1977 and from the Postgraduate School of the Moscow State University in 1980. From 1981 to 1985, he worked for the Institute of Biology and Physiology of Microorganisms in Puschino. From 1985 to 1988, he worked as the head of the Laboratory for Molecular Genetics at Institute of Biotechnology.

Michael D. Tanner: Tanner is a senior fellow at the Cato Institute in Washington D.C., heading research into a variety of domestic policies with particular emphasis on health care reform, welfare policy, and Social Security. His most recent white paper, "Bad Medicine: A Guide to the Real Costs and Consequences of the New Health Care Law," provides a detailed examination of the Patient Protection and Affordable Care Act (Obamacare) and what it means to taxpayers, workers, physicians, and patients.

Frederik Cyrus Roeder: Roeder is a German health economist and managing director of Healthcare Solutions working in the field of healthcare systems in transition. He serves as a Visiting Professor for Health Management at the Lithuanian University of Health Sciences, Kaunas Lithuania and as a Visiting Professor for Healthcare Management and Economic at Ilia State University, Tbilisi Georgia. He appeared in different international journals and media outlets on various healthcare related topics. He is an Associated Researcher at the Montreal Economic Institute.

[1] Richard Kaufman and John Hardt. The Former Soviet Union in Transition. edited for the United States Congress Joint Economic Committee. 1993

[2] Gzirishvili 1998

[3] P Braveman. 2003

[4] TNO report. 2001

[5] Y. Maltsev. What soviet medicine teaches us? 2012

[6] see: informal payments in Soviet Estonia

[7] Donald Bar

[8] Tido von Schoen-Angerer. Understanding health care in the south Caucasus: examples from Armenia. 1999

[9] Gzirishvili Mataradze. Healthcare reforms in Georgia. 1998

[10] World Bank 1996

[11] Gamkrelidze 2002

[12] Gzirishvili, Mataradze 1998

[13] Gamkrelidze 2002

[14] Chawla 2001

[15] Gakrelidze 2002

[16] World Health Report 2002, WHO.

[17] Falkingham and Hemming, 1999

[18] Georgia, Armenia, Kazakhstan, Ukraine, Moldova, Kyrgyzstan, Russia, and

Belarus

[19] Health Service Utilization in the Former Soviet Union: Evidence from Eight Countries. Balabanova, McKee, et al. (2004).

[20] Jorbenadze, Zoidze and others. Health reform and hospital financing in Georgia. 1999

[21] WHO Regional Office for Europe 2009

[22] WHO Regional Office for Europe 2009
[23] see WHO country profile. 2003

[24] WHO, 2005

[25] From the speech of Georgian Prime Minister Z. Nogaideli. Jan. 2007

[26] Transparency International Georgia. One hundred new hospitals for Georgia: how long will they last? 2008

[27] The resolution of the Government of Georgia #11 as of January 26, 2007

[28] HiT Georgia. 2009

[29] A rayon (pl. raiony) is a type of administrative unit of several post-Soviet countries (such as part of an oblast).

[30] The resolution of the Government of Georgia #110 as of April 10, 2010.

[31] World Bank

[32] WB. Georgia Poverty Assessment. 2011

[33] The resolution of the Government of Georgia #166, July 2007

[34] 10 million USD

[35] HSPA. 2012

[36] The resolution of the Government of Georgia #33 February, 2009

[37] appox. 38 USD

[38] The Order of the Minister of Health №01-18/n, 4 April 2012.

[39] George Gotsadze and others. Reforming sanitary-epidemiological service in Central and Eastern Europe and the former Soviet Union: an exploratory study. 2010

[40] The Georgia Health Utilization and Expenditure Study 2010

[41] OECD

[42] Opportunities in Georgia's Pharmaceutical Sector. 2012

[43] see. Curatio. Main highlights of pharmaceutical price and availability in Georgia 2009-2012

[44] for females – 78.7; for males – 70.0

[45] Georgia NCDC yearbook, 2011

www.ingramcontent.com/pod-product-compliance
Lightning Source LLC
Chambersburg PA
CBHW071812170526
45167CB00003B/1284